Mother, Ellen Anne Lane   Great-granny McNiven   Elder brother, Henry Austin Lane   Granny Barbara Michie

Four generations, circa 1920

MARGARET WALTON was born in Inverness in 1928. Her English father, when in the Royal Navy, had been stationed there and met her mother, who was a postwoman – quite unusual then.

She has two brothers (one eight years older, one eight years younger) and a sister, four years younger. They lived in a rented flat, as did two-thirds of Scots at that time. The flat had a large hall, a living room, one large bedroom, a small scullery and an inside toilet (a luxury). There was no telephone and the family certainly had no car for many years. She was part of a loving and caring family.

At the age of five, she went to an infant school (now demolished, with a bus station in its place) in the centre of the town. As it was too far to walk home, she went to her great-grandmother's flat, which was near the school, for her lunch.

There she was served a variety of home-made soups, accompanied by home-made bread. Everything she has learned about home-made soup stems from that time.

One of her joys was to go with her great-grandmother in Proudfoot's taxi* to Brora, up the east coast from Inverness, to visit a family friend. The husband worked as a keeper of eagles and she remembers holding the birds on the back of her hand – under a leather glove, of course! Alas, there are no longer any eagles there.

At the beginning of the war, her elder brother joined the Cameron Highlanders, as did most of the young men of Inverness. He went to France with the British Expeditionary Force and, in 1940, was among the many that were taken prisoner.

At the age of eleven, Margaret won a bursary and went to the local high school. She had not been there long when her mother became ill and she had to do most of the caring at home, doing shopping and looking after the younger children, especially as her father was not fully fit after serving in the First World War.

At fifteen, she had to leave school and find a job to help with the finances, as her mother had become bedridden and Margaret now became 'mother'. She was able to continue her education at night school.

Thus, she had to feed the family on a very small budget – not easy during wartime rationing. She learned from her mistakes and found that she liked cooking and how to put different ingredients together.

When her mother died, her father's family persuaded him to move with the family back to Surrey, which he did in 1947.

There, Margaret met her husband, John, and they were married in 1954 at St John's Church in Redhill. They have a son, a daughter and three grandchildren. She still enjoys cooking!

---

* Proudfoot's taxi was a one-man taxi service that operated in the 1930s.

Lent Lunches
Without Tears

Lent Lunches
Without Tears

Margaret Walton

ATHENA PRESS
LONDON

ISBN: 978 1 84748 345 4

First published 2008 by
ATHENA PRESS
Queen's House, 2 Holly Road
Twickenham TW1 4EG
United Kingdom

Printed for Athena Press

Acknowledgements

My thanks are due to all those members of the congregation who were regular helpers, including Joan Bambury, Maurice Banks, Pamela Faulkner, Beryl Fox, Eileen Hodges, Audrey Love, Jeanette Silk and Annette Wilson. Also those who set up and cleared away the tables in the hall.

The teams, working to the lists each week, got the preparation down to a fine art and all was completed within the hour. This showed that early, detailed planning is important and that systems such as this work best with people who can be depended upon.

My thanks also to Bill Reed, who provided freshly baked soft rolls week by week.

Finally, my special thanks to my husband, John, for all his encouragement and help with the book.

Contents

Introduction

Lent is the forty-day period of fasting leading up to the feast of Easter, recalling Jesus' forty-day fast in the wilderness. Western Lent begins on Ash Wednesday and ends liturgically on the morning of Holy Thursday, although Lenten penance continues through to Holy Saturday.

Churches observe Lent in different ways. At St Andrew's, a weekly 'Lent lunch' is served as part of our observance. This consists of soup, bread and cheese, followed by tea and coffee. Soup was chosen because it is nourishing, filling and forms part of the day's recommended diet. All monies raised go to charity, chosen by the PCC.

This book gives details of the recipes for the soups served, together with the method used and some general guidance on preparation. They were used at St Andrew's Church, Chippenham, from 1994–2006.

To Keep a True Lent

by Robert Herrick

Although the Protestant Church abandoned many Catholic practices at the Reformation, Queen Elizabeth's government extended the ban on meat from just Friday to Wednesday as well, partly to protect the fishing industry! A generation later, Archbishop Laud tried to reintroduce Catholic practices into the religion of the English. The poet asks about the meaning behind the symbol.

> Is this a fast to keep
>   The larder clean?
>   And clean
> From fat of veals and sheep?
>
> Is it to quit the dish
>   Of flesh, yet still
>   To fill
> The platter high with fish?
>
> It is to fast an hour,
>   Or ragg'd to go,
>   Or show
> A downcast look and sour?
>
> No: 'tis a fast to dole
>   Thy sheaf of wheat,
>   And meat,
> Unto the hungry soul.

It is to fast from strife,
  From old debate
    And hate:
To circumcise thy life.

To show a heart grief-rent;
  To starve thy sin,
    Not bin;
And that's to keep thy Lent.

The Recipes

All these recipes and methods are based on the original ones used by my great-grandmother during my childhood in the Highlands of Scotland and can be modified to cater for vegetarians, diabetics and people with allergies.

All soups should be prepared and cooked the night before, taken off the heat and left to stand overnight.* This improves the quality and flavour of the soup.

Next day, soups can be transported to the venue. Bring soup to boiling point again and simmer for at least 10 minutes.

---

* Soups indicated with an asterisk (*) need not stand overnight.

PEA SOUP *

———o◯o———

Serves 8–10 people

3¼ lb peas (petit pois, if available)

1½ lb streaky bacon, chopped

4 onions, chopped

5 pt stock (vegetable)

Elmlea

Serves 18–20 people

7 lb peas (petit pois, if available)

3 lb streaky bacon, chopped

8 onions, chopped

10 pt stock (vegetable)

Elmlea

———o◯o———

COOKING INSTRUCTIONS

Note: this soup need not stand overnight.

Heat oil of choice in saucepan (e.g. olive oil or Fry Light sunflower oil spray).

Lightly brown bacon and onion, add the peas, stir in the stock, bring to the boil and simmer.

Cook for 1 hour.

Purée when cool.

Pass through sieve if necessary.

Bring back to simmer at venue and add Elmlea just before serving.

LENTIL SOUP

Serves 4–6

8 oz lentils
4 rashers streaky bacon
8 oz smoked garlic sausage
1 large onion
2 carrots
4 sticks of celery
1 lb chopped tomatoes

1½ pt water
1 bay leaf
1 tsp dried basil
½ tsp dried marjoram
Pinch of sugar
Salt and pepper

Serves up to 20

2 lb lentils
12 rashers streaky bacon
2 lb smoked garlic sausage
4 large onions
10 carrots
1 head of celery
3 x 800 g tins chopped
tomatoes

10 pt water
4 bay leaves
3 tsp dried basil
1 tsp dried marjoram
Pinch of sugar
Salt and pepper

COOKING INSTRUCTIONS

Carefully pick out any stones that may be mixed in with the lentils. Rinse lentils well and place in a china dish. Cover with boiling water, cover and leave to soak for one hour. Drain well.

Dice the bacon and sauté gently until it just begins to colour.

Cut the garlic sausages into ¼ in. slices and brown them in the bacon dripping.

Pour off all but 2 tbsp of the fat remaining in the pan and sauté the chopped onion, carrots and celery for 5 minutes or until beginning to soften.

Stir in the chopped tomatoes, water and drained lentils. Add the bacon, garlic sausages, herbs and pinch of sugar.

Bring to the boil, then gently simmer until the lentils are soft, approximately 1 hour.

Season with salt and pepper.

MINESTRONE SOUP

Serves 8–10 people

4 oz kidney beans or 4 oz haricot beans
4 oz French beans or 4 oz sliced runner beans
2 courgettes
1 onion, large, chopped
5 tbsp olive oil or oil of choice
1 clove of garlic, crushed
4 rashers streaky bacon
2 tsp basil
1–2 tsp marjoram
Salt and pepper
4 pts stock(see p.65)
4 oz fresh peas or frozen
5 carrots, chopped
8 oz tomatoes, chopped
3–4 stalks of celery, chopped
1 small cabbage, shredded
5 oz macaroni
Parmesan cheese, grated

Serves up to 20 people

8 oz haricot beans or 8 oz kidney beans
8 oz French beans or sliced runner beans
8 onions, chopped
10 tbsp olive oil or oil of choice
6 cloves of garlic, crushed
12 rashers streaky bacon
Salt and pepper
10 pt stock (see page 65)
10 large carrots, sliced
3 lb tomatoes
12 oz chopped celery
3 lb shredded cabbage
10 oz macaroni
Parmesan cheese, grated

COOKING INSTRUCTIONS

Soak kidney beans and haricot beans in water overnight (see 'pulses', p.65), ready to cook the following day.

The next day, heat oil of choice and toss in the onions, garlic, bacon, drained pulses and stock. Add seasoning.

Cook for 1½ hours.

Add carrots, tomatoes and remaining green vegetables (except the cabbage).

Cook for another 20 minutes, adding a little stock if necessary.

Leave to stand overnight for the flavours to blend.

The next day take to the venue and bring back to the boil for a few minutes, then simmer.

10 minutes before serving add the cabbage and macaroni (no earlier or they will be overcooked) and add more salt and pepper if necessary.

A little red wine may be added at this stage and the soup may also be sprinkled with a little Parmesan cheese if desired.

BROCCOLI SOUP *

Serves 8–10 people

4 large heads of broccoli, chopped
4 large onions, chopped

Vegetable stock to cover
Elmlea
Salt and pepper as required

Serves 16–20 people

8 large heads of broccoli, chopped
8 large onions, chopped

Vegetable stock to cover
Elmlea
Salt and pepper as required

COOKING INSTRUCTIONS

Place chopped veg in the pan and cover with vegetable stock.

Cook for 1 hr.

Add salt and pepper.

Purée when cool.

Bring back to simmer at venue.

Add Elmlea just before serving.

23

CELERY SOUP *

Serves 8–10 people

5 tbsp oil	*5 pt water*
5 medium heads celery	*5 rashers streaky bacon*
3 medium potatoes	*Salt and pepper*
3 medium onions	*2 tbsp fresh fennel, chopped*
2 cloves garlic	*and set aside for garnish*

Serves 16 20 people

10 tbsp oil	*10 pt water*
10 medium heads celery	*10 rashers streaky bacon*
6 medium potatoes	*Salt and pepper*
6 medium onions	*4 tbsp fresh fennel, chopped*
4 cloves garlic	*and set aside for garnish*

COOKING INSTRUCTIONS

Chop all the remaining vegetables and sweat in oil, i.e. slightly brown, for 5 minutes.

Add water and cook for 15–20 minutes.

Liquidise when cool.

Season with salt and pepper.

Garnish with freshly chopped fennel (if liked).

TOMATO SOUP

———○◯○———

Serves 4–6 people

1 small carrot	*¼ tsp salt*
1 small onion	*3 shakes of pepper*
1–2 oz streaky bacon	*1 bouquet garni*
½ oz margarine	*Small amount of basil*
Splash of Worcester sauce	*¾ oz plain flour or corn-*
1 Kallo chicken stock cube	*flour*
1 x 14 oz tin of tomatoes	*¼ pt milk*
with juice	

For 16–20 persons

4 carrots	*1 tsp salt*
4 onions	*9 shakes pepper*
½ lb streaky bacon	*2 bouquet garnis*
2 oz margarine	*Small amount of basil*
Splash of Worcester sauce	*3 oz plain flour or cornflour*
4 Kallo chicken stock cubes	*1 pt milk*
4 x 14 oz tins of tomatoes	
with juice	

NB: Always use plain flour or cornflour for all thickening purposes as self-raising flour does not blend in smoothly.

———○◯○———

COOKING INSTRUCTIONS

Dice carrots, onion and bacon.

Sauté vegetables by placing margarine and bacon squares into pan and heat slowly until the fat melts completely, then add the carrot, onion and Worcester sauce and stir.

Cook on low heat until the vegetables have absorbed the fat and then remove from heat.

Make up stock by adding stock cube to tomato juice from tinned tomatoes and make up to 1 pt with boiling water and add to vegetables.

Add tomatoes, salt, pepper, basil and bouquet garnis.

Return to heat and simmer for 10–20 minutes with lid partly on. (Place long-handled wooden stirring spoon across top of pan about 1 " from edge, place lid on top leaving an air gap under spoon.)

Mix flour and milk until smooth.

Remove bouquet garni and liquidate soup.

Add thickening, stir soup quickly and return to medium heat for 3 minutes.

POTATO AND LEEK SOUP

———○○○———

Serves 4–6 people

1 lb potatoes, peeled and chopped
1 large onion, peeled and chopped
2 bay leaves
2 oz oil
1½ lb leeks, slit the green part, wash under running water, shake well and slice into rings
1½ pt stock (vegetable)
Salt and pepper
¼ pt milk
½–1 tsp nutmeg
¼ pt cream (single)

Serves 12–14 people

9 lb potatoes, peeled and chopped
6 onions, peeled and chopped
6 bay leaves
5 lb leeks, slit the green parts, wash under running water, shake well and slice into rings
8 pt stock (vegetable)
Salt and pepper
2¼ pt milk
1–4 tsp nutmeg
2¼ pt cream (single)
4 oz oil

———○○○———

COOKING INSTRUCTIONS

Sauté potatoes and onions with bay leaf in oil for 5 minutes.

Add sliced leeks and cook for another 3–4 minutes.

Pour in vegetable stock and add salt and pepper to taste.

Bring to the boil and cook for 20 minutes.

Allow to cool slightly.

Blend batches in blender until smooth and return to clean pan.

Blend in milk and nutmeg.

Stir well and taste for correct seasoning.

Add cream before serving.

CARROT AND CORIANDER SOUP

---○○○---

Serves 6 people

12 oz carrots
1 Spanish onion
1 clove of garlic, if liked
2 tbsp sunflower oil
3 level tsp ground coriander
2 level tsp ground cumin

1 level tsp turmeric
1 cooking apple
1–1½ pt stock (vegetable)
Salt and pepper
¼ pt Elmlea

Serves 20 people

9 lb carrots
8 Spanish onions
12 cloves of garlic, if liked
16 tbsp sunflower oil
4 level tbsp ground coriander

2 level tsp cumin
2 level tsp turmeric
8 large cooking apples
10 pt stock (vegetable)
Salt and pepper
2 tubs of Elmlea

---○○○---

COOKING INSTRUCTIONS

Peel and chop carrots, onions and garlic.

Heat oil in a pan, add vegetables and fry gently for 10 minutes.

Stir in spices and cook gently for further 2 minutes, stirring well.

Chop apple and add with stock. Simmer for 40–45 minutes.

Allow to cool slightly, then purée.

Sieve into rinsed pan, add salt and pepper and then bring to boil at venue. If it thickens too much, add warm water.

Stir in Elmlea and serve piping hot.

CURRIED CREAM OF CAULIFLOWER SOUP *

Serves 6–10 people

¼ lb butter	2 oz plain flour
½ lb onions, peeled and finely sliced	2 pt chicken stock
	1 pt creamy milk
2 lb prepared cauliflower	4 bay leaves
1 level tbsp curry powder	Salt and pepper

Serves 12–20 people

½ lb butter	4 pt chicken stock
1 lb onions, peeled and finely sliced	2 pt creamy milk
	6 bay leaves
4 lb prepared cauliflower	Salt and pepper
1 level tbsp curry powder	
4 oz plain flour	

COOKING INSTRUCTIONS

Melt butter in a saucepan. Stir in onion and cook, stirring occasionally until tender.

Roughly chop the cauliflower and add to pan. Cover with a tightly fitting lid and cook for a further 15–20 minutes, stirring occasionally.

Add curry powder, return the pan to the heat and cook over a gentle heat for 2–3 minutes; add the flour and cook for a few minutes longer.

Make up stock and add to pan with milk and bay leaves. Bring to the boil, cover and simmer for 45 minutes.

Discard the bay leaves and adjust the seasoning.

Purée the soup in an electric blender.

KING'S SPICED PARSNIP SOUP

Serves 6 people

3 fl oz oil (sunflower)
1 lb onions, chopped
1½ lb parsnips, chopped
1 clove of garlic, if liked
2–2½ pt stock (vegetable)
Salt and pepper
1 rounded tsp curry powder

1 tsp cumin
1 tsp cardamom
1 tsp turmeric
pinch of ginger
¼ pt Elmlea single cream
1 lb cooking apples

Serves 20 people

12 fl oz oil (sunflower)
3 lb onions, chopped
9 lb parsnips, chopped
4 cloves garlic, if liked
10 pt stock (vegetable)
Salt and pepper
4 rounded tsp curry powder

2 tsp cumin
2 tsp cardamom
2 tsp turmeric
pinch of ginger
1 pt Elmlea single cream
4 lb apples

COOKING INSTRUCTIONS

Heat the oil and add onions, parsnips and garlic.

Fry for 5 minutes, then blend in the stock and the salt and pepper and bring to the boil, stirring all the while.

Simmer for ½–1 hour and then test the parsnips.

Purée the soup until smooth, then reheat until piping hot.

Taste and check the seasoning.

Add cream (do not let the soup boil after adding cream).

SCOTCH BROTH

———○○○———

Serves 6–10 people

4 oz barley (soaked over-night)
8 oz split peas (soaked overnight)
½ shoulder of lamb (small)
3 carrots
1 medium swede (not turnip)

5 leeks
5 potatoes
Salt and pepper
1 lb frozen peas
6 pt water (no need for stock if using fresh lamb)

Serves up to 20 people

8 oz barley (soaked over-night)
16 oz split peas (soaked overnight)
½ shoulder lamb (large)
6 carrots
2 medium Swedes (not turnip)

10 leeks
10 potatoes
Salt and pepper
2 lb frozen peas
12 pt water (no need for stock if using fresh lamb)

———○○○———

COOKING INSTRUCTIONS

Strain soaked pulses, rinse and place in clean pan. Cover with fresh water and simmer for 6 minutes.

Strain and place in large pan with 6 pt water (12 pt for double recipe) and add the lamb. Boil for 2 hours. Remove lamb shoulder from pan.

Wash, peel and chop carrots, swede and white of leeks. Add to pan with pulses. Cook for 40 minutes.

Remove the meat from the bone and set aside.

Next day, finely chop green of leeks, dice potatoes and add both to pan. Add reserved meat.

Season well with salt and pepper and cook for a further 20 minutes.

Add peas for last 10 minutes.

Serve immediately, piping hot.

CHICKEN SOUP

———○◯○———

Serves 5–6 people

1 roasted chicken	*1 bouquet garni*
Salt and pepper	*2 oz cornflour*
1–2 onions	*Fried croutons to garnish*
1–2 carrots	*2 chicken stock cubes*

———○◯○———

COOKING INSTRUCTIONS

Remove skin and meat from roasted chicken and put meat to one side. Retain carcass. Discard skin.

To make the stock, put the chicken carcass plus giblets, if available, into a large pan (but not the liver as it gives too strong a flavour). Cover with water; add seasoning, vegetables, herbs and stock cubes.

Bring to boil, cover the pan and simmer for at least 2 hours.

Remove carcass, giblets and bouquet garni.

Next day at the venue, add the cooked chicken pieces to the pan.

Blend the cornflour with a little cold stock or milk. Place in pan, bring to boil and stir well until thickened.

Serve with croutons.

CHICKEN AND LEEK SOUP

For 12–20 persons

4 tbsp oil
8 rashers of bacon
6 sticks of celery, cut up
6 lb leeks
12 pt chicken stock (using cubes)

1 lb barley (see 'pulses', p.65)
4 tsp salt and pepper
1 roasted chicken, meat removed

COOKING INSTRUCTIONS

Heat oil in pan. Add bacon and celery and fry gently for 5 minutes until bacon is crisp.

Wash leeks thoroughly and cut into 1 inch lengths. Add half to pan and cook for 2 minutes.

Add stock made with stock cube and water.

Add barley and salt and pepper.

Simmer gently for 1 hour.

Stir in remaining leeks and meat and cook for a further 30–40 minutes.

CHICKEN NOODLE SOUP

———o○o———

Serves 5–6 people

1 small roasted chicken
4 onions, chopped
6 carrots, chopped
2 bouquet garnis
1 small tube of tomato paste
2 lb petit pois peas

Salt and pepper
2 tbsp cornflour, slaked with milk
1 lb pasta
6 pts chicken stock, made from stock cubes

Serves 10–20 people

1 roasted chicken
8 onions, chopped
12 carrots, chopped
3 bouquet garnis
1 large tube of tomato paste
Salt and pepper

4 lb petit pois peas
4 tbsp cornflour, slaked with milk
1 lb pasta
12 pts chicken stock, made from stock cubes

———o○o———

COOKING INSTRUCTIONS

Remove skin and meat from roasted chicken and put to one side. Retain carcass. Discard skin.

To make the stock, put the chicken carcass plus giblets, if available, into a large pan (but not the liver as it gives too strong a flavour). Cover with water.

Remove carcass and giblets, bring stock to boil, then add onions, carrots, bouquet garnis, tomato paste and salt and pepper.

Simmer for 2 hours.

Next day at venue, bring back to boil, add peas and simmer for a further 15 minutes. Switch off the heat.

Add cornflour slaked with milk[*]. Stir well.

Add chicken pieces and pasta and simmer for 10 minutes before serving.

Serve piping hot.

---

[*] To 'slake', add ½ pint milk to cornflour to make a thickening agent and stir well until thickened and creamy.

MULLIGATAWNY SOUP

Serves up to 20 people

8 oz unsalted butter (or oil)	*1 tbsp Madras curry*
8–10 oz pre-cooked chicken	*powder*
5 chopped cooking apples	*10 pt stock (lamb)*
5 medium onions, peeled	*16 tbsp basmati rice*
and finely chopped	*Salt and pepper*
16 tomatoes, seeded and	*4 tbsp mango chutney*
chopped (seeds discarded)	

COOKING INSTRUCTIONS

Melt butter or heat oil and add chicken, apple and onion to pan. Brown lightly.

Add tomatoes, sprinkle over curry powder and continue to brown. Be careful not to burn the vegetables here.

Add stock, bring to boil.

Lower heat and simmer for 40 minutes.

Leave overnight for the flavours to blend.

At venue, add rice, bring to boil and cook for 12 minutes before serving.

NB: This recipe can be adapted to serve any number of people by altering the amount of ingredients by an appropriate proportion.

CULLEN SKINK

Cullen skink is probably Scotland's most enjoyed fish soup. The fish used in a traditional cullen skink is Finnan haddock, but this is hard to find across the Scottish–English border. When unavailable, use undyed smoked haddock fillets. There is more than one recipe for this soup. Here is my version.

Serves 5–6 people

2 Finnan haddock or 18 oz undyed smoked haddock fillets

2 onions, peeled and finely chopped

1¼ lb potatoes, peeled and finely diced

Pepper (to taste)

16 oz full-fat milk

1 oz unsalted butter

Double cream and chopped chives to garnish

COOKING INSTRUCTIONS

Put the haddock into a pan with 12 oz water. Bring to boil and simmer for 9–10 minutes.

Add onions and potatoes to the pan. If the vegetables are not covered with water, add a little of the milk.

Add some pepper (salt may not be required as fish is a bit salty, taste first).

Cover pan with lid and simmer for 15 minutes.

Remove pan from the heat and mash the contents. Nowadays, I use a blender, but the soup must be cool before blending.

Add the milk and butter.

Bring to boil and simmer for 5 minutes.

Add the fish and reheat gently for 10 minutes.

Make sure that the plates are hot and swirl with a little cream and chives before serving.

Organisation

Timing

The leader, three helpers and all the food previously prepared by the leader should be in the venue by 11.30 a.m. for serving at 12.30 p.m.

Requirements for the Kitchen:

Cutlery – soup spoons and knives wrapped in napkins and placed on a large tray

Soup bowls

Teapots and large coffee jugs

Large plates

Teaspoons

Milk jugs

Tea towels to cover the bread

Salt and pepper pots

Bread boards and bread knives

Paper napkins

Rubber gloves

Plastic bags to cover the bread

Cheese knives

Baskets for the bread and the cheeses

Ladles for the soup

Refuse bags

Money bowl

Hot plate

Notice for cost

Large wooden spoons

Dishes for pickle

Glasses for drinking water

Sugar basins

Weekly Shopping List[*]

Bread can be made at home using a bread machine and Carrs flour, both white and wholemeal. Any left over from this bread makes wonderful toast.

17 loaves, including white and brown

Soft rolls

Soup ingredients with 12–14 pt stock

5 lb cheese (including a vegetarian alternative)

2 large boxes of butter pats

Chutney and pickle

Traidcraft instant coffee and tea

Sugar cubes

6 pt milk

Gluten-free biscuits

Fresh drinking water

Paper tablecloths

---

[*] To cater for up to 40 people, which can be adjusted to suit the situation

Dos and Don'ts

Dos	Don'ts
Do purchase 2 heavy-duty unpolished aluminium pans, size 10.2 litres. The contents do not require constant stirring.	Don't purchase stainless steel pans, because you will have to continually stir the contents.
Post notice on board calling for volunteers – three plus co-ordinator. Remember the saying, 'too many cooks spoil the broth'.	Packet soup is not recommended because of additives. Most of the customers are elderly.
Always make soup using fresh ingredients.	Do guard against many people bringing small quantities of soup. This causes problems with keeping it hot and with the collection and return of the containers.
It is useful, if possible, that all helpers arrive on time.	

Duties for the Helpers at the Venue

The three helpers to meet at the venue at 11.30 a.m. and set out items as under:			
Helper No.1	Helper No.2	Helper No.3	Leader
40 large plates	cutlery	cut bread	1 kettle for tea
40 large soup bowls to be heated	wrap soup spoons & knives in napkins	gluten-free biscuits	1 kettle for coffee
Fill 2 milk jugs	teaspoons	cut cheeses	coffee
Fill 2 sugar basins	1 tray for cutlery	baskets for the bread and butter	tea
salt and pepper	fill 4 dishes with pickles	2 bread knives	soup
water jug & water		bags to keep the bread covered	matches
		spread margarine	2 ladles
			2 wooden spoons
			1 bowl for money

Example of a Notice Calling for Volunteers

Three volunteers are needed to help with the Lent Lunches once weekly on the chosen day, to be at the venue at 11.30 a.m. Would those willing to help please enter their name and telephone number below:

		1	*2*	*3*
Date	*Name* *Tel. no.*			
Date	*Name* *Tel. no.*			
Date	*Name* *Tel. no.*			
Date	*Name* *Tel. no.*			
Date	*Name* *Tel. no.*			
Date	*Name* *Tel. no.*			

Hygiene Sense

For people involved in catering in the UK, it is essential that they obtain a Food Hygiene Options Certificate as issued by the Chartered Institute of Environmental Health, who also recommend that refresher training be undertaken every three years.

Various organisations provide training courses and details of the nearest one can be obtained from your Local Authority.

Bacteria

Bacteria need the right type of food, including moisture, the correct temperature (ideally between 20 °C and 50 °C) and sufficient time in order to live and grow. Some food poisoning bacteria can reproduce every ten minutes.

High-risk Foods

High-risk foods are ready-to-eat foods which support the multiplication of food-poisoning bacteria and will be eaten without cooking or other treatment which would destroy any bacteria that may be present. They are usually stored under refrigeration and must be kept apart from raw foods. They include cooked meat and poultry, gravy, dairy produce, seafood and cooked rice.

Bacterial Contamination

Bacteria are transferred from the source to high-risk foods by hands, clothes and equipment, as well as hand-contact surfaces and food-contact surfaces. Cross-contamination is the transfer of bacteria from contaminated foods (usually raw) to other foods.

Preventing Food Poisoning

- During preparation, keep food at room temperature for the shortest possible time.
- Keep food hot or cold to avoid conditions for bacteria to grow.
- Destroy the bacteria in the food by thorough cooking.

Personal Hygiene

Food poisoning organisms can be spread by sneezing, coughing or touching high-risk foods. Proper hand-washing, i.e. washing wrists, nails, between fingers, etc. is essential to prevent the spread of bacteria.

Cleaning and Disinfection

This is required:

- to remove matter upon which bacteria could grow,
- to reduce the risk of foreign matter contamination,
- to comply with the law.

Use of Refrigerator

Keep raw food and high-risk foods separate and store high-risk food above raw food. Temperature inside the refrigerator should be below 5 °C.

Handling Frozen Poultry

Keep this separate from other foods. Thaw completely in a cool room. Once thawed, keep in a refrigerator and cook within twenty-four hours.

Temperatures

Cooking temperature should be above 75 °C.

Hot holding temperature should be above 63 °C.

Danger zone for rapid bacterial growth is 20–50 °C.

Chill temperature is 1–4 °C.

CONVERSION TABLES

Notes on Metrication

Imperial measures have been used throughout this book. The metric equivalents given below have been calculated to the nearest twenty-five-gram step for weight and fifty-millilitre step for liquid measures. Some adjustments may be necessary when using the metric measurements.

Weights		Liquid Measure	
Ounces	Grams	Imperial	Metric (ml)
½	15	1 tsp	5
1	25	1 tbsp	15
2	50	1 fl oz	25
3	75	2 fl oz	50
4	125	4 fl oz	100
5	150	5 fl oz	150
6	175	10 fl oz	300
7	200	20 fl oz (1 pt)	600
8	250	35 fl oz (1¾ pt)	1000 (1 litre)
9	275		
10	300		
12	375		
16 (1 lb)	500		

Notes on American and Australian Measures

In America, the 8 oz measuring cup is used, while in Australia metric measures are used in conjunction with the standard 250 ml measuring cup.

The imperial pint used in Britain and Australia is 20 fl oz, while the American pint is 16 fl oz.

The British standard tablespoon holds 17.7 ml, the American 14.2 ml and the Australian 20 ml. A teaspoon holds approximately 5 ml in all three countries. A pinch is universally about ¼ teaspoonful.

Glossary

PCC	Parochial Church Council
Elmlea	a trade name for a blend of buttermilk and vegetable oils, supplied as double and single (light).
pulses	please check the labels for store-cupboard life and follow soaking time as recommended. Most pulses have to be soaked to replace moisture, so start cooking them the day before making the soup. Cover with water, bring to the boil, simmer for 6 minutes, then leave to soak overnight. Next day, rinse well in fresh water and add to casserole or pan before starting to cook for 2 hours.
	List of pulses: butter beans, red kidney beans, haricot beans, soya beans, aduki beans, lentils, split peas, dried peas, chick peas.
stock cubes	recommended are:

1. Marigold: Swiss vegetable bouillon – gluten-free and without preservatives, colouring, artificial flavouring or GM materials.
2. Kallo: organic stock cubes available in chicken, tomato and herb, garlic and herb, French onion, beef, premium beef, organic mushroom, organic vegetable, premium vegetable and low salt vegetable. No artificial additives are included.

flour	Carrs: my preferred choice of flour, available in strong white and brown, good for use in a bread-making machine.
'I can't believe it's not butter'	a butter substitute.
Traidcraft	the trade name for the churches' charity.

Alphabetical List of Soups